The Sun Has Burned My Skin

The Sun Has Burned My Skin

a modest paraphrase
of solomon's song of songs

Adam S. Miller
2017

The Sun Has Burned My Skin:
A Modest Paraphrase of Solomon's Song of Songs

© 2017 Adam S. Miller

21 20 19 18 17   1 2 3 4 5

ISBN-10: 0-9986052-5-5
ISBN-13: 978-0-9986052-5-8

For information, contact:
By Common Consent Press
4062 South Evelyn Drive
Salt Lake City, Utah 84124-2250

www.bccpress.org

This text for this book uses Warnock Pro, designed by Robert Slimbach for Adobe and released in 2000. The titles are set in Frutiger, created by Adrian Frutiger and released by Stempel with Linotype in 1976.

Cover and book design by Jenny Webb
www.jennywebbedits.com

For Gwen

CONTENTS

The Eden story preserves a memory of wholeness and abundance from the beginning of time; the prophets look forward to a peaceable kingdom at the End of Days. The Song of Songs locates that kingdom in human love, in the habitable present, and for the space of our attention, allows us to enter it.

—Ariel and Chana Bloch

INTRODUCTION

Solomon's Song of Songs is canonized erotica. It's scripture about sex. But the Song of Songs isn't just about sex. It's also about love. The Song of Songs is about what happens when a billion years of blind, reproductive pressure gets packed inside the fragile walls of a single human body—and, then, it's about what happens when this blind pressure is alchemically paired with the disarming specificity of an enduring love for just one other person. The book's poetry performs this same kind of alchemy. It matches its frank eroticism with innocence and tenderness. If you see only the former, you'll be lost. If you can bear only the latter, I wish you well.

Though there are many kinds of love, the Song of Songs gives voice to just one experience of it. It unfolds over the course of eight chapters through a series of interwoven songs as a conversation between a woman and a man. The woman's voice leads and calls. The man's voice praises and responds. The book's authorship and date of composition are unclear. But, as André LaCocque and others have argued, the book may have been composed by a woman.[1] In either case, as received, it is the only book in our canon that is narrated principally—and in the first person— by a woman's voice.

The songs narrate moments of union, parting, and, especially, the desire that bridges them. Sex is at the heart of each of these moments. As a noun, sex names the (oft enumerated) physical differences that fascinate the singers. As a verb, sex names the (oft alluded to) erotic act that joins them. In both respects, the songs are grounded, earthy, and pastoral. They are concrete and sen-

---

1. See André LaCocque, *Romance She Wrote: A Hermeneutical Essay on Song of Songs* (Eugene, OR: Wipf and Stock Publishers, 2006), 39–53.

sual. They lean into images that evoke tastes and fragrances. They linger in their appreciation of a curve or a blush. But for all their interest in appearances, the songs never feel superficial. Rather, they pulse with energy. Every lovingly admired surface—every apparently stable quality, property, and predicate—hardly veils the power at work beneath it.

When this veil grows thin, sex can expose us not only to the love and desire of another person, it can expose us to the raw truth of being human. It can expose us to the truth that beyond all of the polished surfaces, perfected images, and fixed essences with which we ceaselessly try to identify, we are more fundamentally a live power than a finished thing.

At the crossroads of blind drive and enduring devotion, sex unmasks us. It unmakes us. It shows us to one another—and to ourselves—as paper-thin fictions, as vulnerable bodies, as intimate strangers, as unfinished things. It shows us to each other as uncanny powers to love, to make love, and to make life. Sex, rather than abolishing this strangeness, shares it. And then, naked and trembling and shared, something crucial about God's own strangeness and vulnerability—something crucial about what it means to be *alive* in Christ—can also blink into view.

Or, at least, it might.

Unfinished as we are, sometimes this specific kind of alchemy doesn't happen. Sometimes sex and love fail to coincide. Sometimes there's just sex. Sometimes there's just love. Sometimes there's neither. Sometimes, instead of falling unmade into someone else's arms, we just end up wrecked by someone else's fall—or, even, by our own.

These possibilities crowd the margins of the Song, just off the page, just out of sight. But the Song itself is something else. The Song of Songs is, unapologetically, a celebration of what happens when lives do cross and love is made.

BACKGROUND

As with my work on Ecclesiastes and Romans, what follows is not a translation. It is a loose paraphrase that aims more for the replication of a certain mood than for the correspondence of particular words and phrases. Be aware that I frequently bend and reshape the text's own images. Working with these songs, I found that they were too intimate and personal not to take personally. A strange, hybrid fruit resulted. The songs are themselves a collection of age-old Israelite love songs, searing and intense, sung principally by a young woman who is bold, confident, and only just exposed to the tidal pull of love and sex. But what you'll find in this paraphrase is something else. What you'll get here is that ancient, feminine voice refracted through the heart of a long-married, middle-aged, bourgeois, first-world, twenty-first century white guy with literary pretensions and three kids. Such refraction comes with real costs. My renderings are, inevitably, skewed by my masculinity and tinged by my domesticity. Important parts of the original are lost along the way. However, despite the great distance between us, I refuse to believe that these songs cannot still ring in my own heart and mind. I refuse to believe that these are songs I cannot, at least in part, sing.

Still, be aware of these blind spots. Be aware of the costs. The song is itself attuned to them and, often, has a polemical edge that both subtly and overtly pushes back against both sexism and prudery. As Ariel and Chana Bloch note:

> In the Bible, written for the most part from a male point of view, women are by definition the second sex. History is traced through the line of the fathers, as in priestly genealogies ("And Enoch begat Methuselah"), and the typical formulas for sexual relations ("he knew her," "he came into her," "he lay with her") make the woman seem passive and acted upon. But in the Song, where the lovers take turns inviting one another, desire is entirely reciprocal. Both are described in images that suggest tenderness (lilies, doves, gazelles) as well as strength and stateliness (pillars, towers). In this book of the Bible, the woman is certainly the

equal of the man. Indeed, she often seems more than his equal.[2]

This kind of equality and reciprocity between the sexes is, in scripture, alarmingly rare.

The history of the Song's interpretation is long and complex. Given its marginal status in Mormonism, readers may be surprised to learn that the Song of Songs is traditionally among the most commented upon and elaborately dissected books of the Bible.

Responses to the book have varied widely. Some interpreters found the songs to be profoundly offensive. They regarded the book's celebration of *eros* as little more than pornography and recommended that chaste readers staple their biblical pages shut. Conversely, some interpreters have celebrated what they see as the godless, earthy, and irreligious "secularity" of the songs, noting that these songs are, after all, about sex, that the couple is likely unmarried, and that God

2. Ariel Bloch and Chana Bloch, *The Song of Songs: A New Translation with an Introduction and Commentary* (New York: Random House, 1995), 4.

is not invoked. However, most of the book's interpreters adopted a different approach. These songs,
they claimed, are not *actually* about sex. Rather,
these songs are a thinly veiled allegory. They are
a code to be cracked that, properly interpreted,
can instruct us about spiritual truths far removed
from the troubles of the flesh. They can teach us
what it means for Israel to be loved by God or for
the church to be the bride of Christ.

For my part, I find each of these traditional
approaches incomplete and often unconvincing.
However, it seems to me that André LaCocque's
recent account of the Song opens a way forward. LaCocque argues that the book's songs are
straightforwardly a celebration of the human experience of love and sex. But he also argues that
they are, at the same time, deeply religious. While
the songs are not allegorical, they do, he contends,
intentionally and persistently *reappropriate* biblical language and prophetic metaphors used else-
where. Where Israel's prophets adapted the pro-
fane language of marital intimacy to describe the
sacred character of Israel's relationship to God,
these songs work to systematically bend that now

prophetic language back around to describe human love itself as sacred and divine.

> The very use of prophetic metaphors for the singing of the loves between a man and a woman reflects back upon the prophetic sources, shedding new light upon them. Prophets insisted upon the relationship between God and Israel as metaphorically nuptial. No sooner has that metaphor traveled back down to characterize the relationship between a man and a woman in the Song than it ricochets again and human eros is endowed with a vertical dimension that ennobles it and makes of it the prime translation in life of the *imago Dei*. When this is realized, it becomes clear why the prophets chose *that* metaphor in the first place.[3]

Passing the image of ordinary human love through the machinery of prophetic language imprinted those intimate images with a divine di-

3. LaCocque, *Romance She Wrote: A Hermeneutical Essay on Song of Songs*, 65.

mension. The Song of Songs, then, takes advantage of this new dimension by reapplying these now prophetic images to ordinary human love.

NOTES

In preparing my own paraphrase, I referred primarily to the King James Version, the New English Translation, and Ariel and Chana Bloch's excellent translation.[4] I occasionally but rarely referred to the original Hebrew text. In general, my renderings pare the original text to the bone. I narrowed the scope of the songs to just the dialogue between the woman and the man and filtered out occasional asides made to "the daughters of Jerusalem" and others. I also basically followed Ariel and Chana Bloch's assignation of particular songs to particular speakers. As a rule, I simplified the images and strove for a more modest, naturalistic tone in order to pre-

4. Ariel Bloch and Chana Bloch, *The Song of Songs: A New Translation with an Introduction and Commentary.*

vent the language from obscuring, for a contemporary sensibility, the heart of the songs.

There is nothing remotely definitive about what I offer here. Treat this paraphrase as a beginning, not an end. Take it as a tease, as an incitement, as an invitation to study the songs themselves in a variety of parallel translations and, wherever possible, in the original Hebrew. More, take the obvious weakness of my own attempt as an invitation to try producing your own.

SONG OF SONGS 1

The Woman

1–4

Kiss me.
Not just once, brushing past.
Not just a taste,
but the whole bottle of wine.

I catch your scent
clinging to a shirt or
a still warm sheet—

No wonder, I murmur,
women wander after you.

Hurry—take my hand.
Forget the sun
and come back to bed.

The Woman

4–6

My skin is dark like the earth.

You kiss my bare shoulder,
wondering why—

The sun has burned my skin!

The Woman

6

> Fear and shame conspire
> to lock away my heart
> and bar the vineyard.
>
> But try as I might,
> I can't forget
> the lingering taste of wine.

The Woman

Why do you make my blood pound
and then, when I reach for you, vanish?

Where do you go?
What lost sheep are you looking for?
In what shade do you hide?

Don't leave me to circle idly
into the disappointment
of someone else's arms!

The Man

Where have I gone?
If you don't know,
follow the footprints
I left in the dark earth.

Come, fold your flocks with mine.
Rest in the shepherd's tent.

9–10

The Man

You sit like pharaoh,
just out of reach,
at the heart of my dreams.

When next I see you,
I whisper the dream
in your ear,
the tip of my finger
on the small of your back.

You blush?
Color spreads across your cheeks
and down your breastbone,
lovely with a string of pearls.

The Woman

>Lay close beside me.
>Don't go hungry,
>the table is set.

13–14

The Woman

> I fear everyone I meet
> will catch the scent of you
> lingering on my hands,
> between my breasts,
> tattooed like blossoms
> up and down my arms.

The Man

>	Your careless beauty ruins me—
>	your hands, your eyes, aflutter.

16–17

The Woman

Hand in hand under an open sky, we're home.
These leaves make our bed,
these trees frame our room,
these branches cover our heads.

Quick—we're already home.

SONG OF SONGS 2

The Woman

> I am the rose of Sharon.
> I am the lily of the valleys.

The Man

2

You are a flower
in a field of thistles.

The Woman

You are an apple tree
in a forest of pines.

I tuck into the shade of your boughs,
the tang of fruit on my tongue.

The Woman

4–6

You usher me into the house of wine,
bannered by love.

My head spins and
my knees are weak.

You lift me into bed,
press a damp cloth to my brow,
cool against the heat
—I shiver.

You nurse me
when love's fever grips me.
With one hand you cradle my head,
with one hand you pull me close.

The Woman

Swear to me—
You won't wake love before its time.

The Woman

Listen—I hear you calling.
Look—I see you coming.
Tireless, crossing mountains
and risking seas.

Already you're through the gate
and at the door.

How long did you
stand there in the night,
reflected in the window,
watching me
waiting for you?

The Man

10–13

> Give me the key
> and come away.
>
> The ice is cracking,
> winter is passed.
>
> Flowers bloom,
> robins sing,
> trees bud,
> and vines entwine the gate.

The Man

Don't hide like a dove
in the cleft of a rock,
in the shy darkness
of a lampless night.

Take off your mask.
Let me see your bright eyes.
Let me hear your low voice
whisper my name.

The Woman

15–16

> Don't let the foxes
> raid our vineyard
> and spoil the wine.

> You are mine
> and I am yours
> alone.

The Woman

Day breaks
and shadows flee.

Now that you've seen me
in the full light of day—
will you stay?

The Woman

1–5

> All night long,
> I lay alone
> trying to remember
> the weight of you.
>
> But you never came.
>
> Restless, I looked for you.
> I drifted out the door
> and down the street.
>
> I stopped caring what others—
> restless themselves?
> watching from their windows?
> —might think or say.

I needed you.

When you finally came
through the door,
I didn't wait.

The Woman

5

Swear to me again—
You won't wake love before its time.

The Woman

Who are you?

Who could this be
stumbling in from the heat of the desert,
wild, smoky, and bruised?

Are you a caravan of spices?
A mirage?
A daydream?

Who are these warriors
that surround you,
trained in the art of war,
their swords bright?

Why all these trophies—
the exotic wood,
the purple wool,
the inlaid jewels
—that pull you away
and delay your return?

Why be like Solomon?
Let me be your crown.

The Man

You are beautiful.

I wake early to watch you sleep—

The lock of hair tucked behind your ear,
the laugh lines around your eyes,
your crooked tooth and parted lips,

how the sheet clings
in the gray morning light
to the curve of your hip.

I lay my head on your breast and
listen to your heart,
your breath warm on my neck.

You stir and pull me closer.

The Man

Leave the mountain heights.
Come with me into the valley,
away from the leopards
and dens of lions.

The Man

My heart beats
in your breast.

When first I saw you
I couldn't look away.

Your necklace,
the hem of your dress,
the smile in your eyes,
the scent of your perfume—
musk, a hint of citrus.

You leaned close
and kissed me,
milk and honey
under your tongue.

I forgot my own name.

The Man

You are a secret garden,
a hidden well,
a sealed spring.

Behind your walls,
affections grow
and intentions take root—
pomegranates,
cinnamon,
saffron,
sunflowers,
and cane.

Hidden in the garden's nave,
a fountain wells with life.

The Woman

Let the winds blow
and the seasons change.

Let these spices
fill the air and drift,
redolent,
beyond the garden walls.

Can you catch the scent
of a summer harvest?

The Man

> We dance in the garden
> and gather its fruit.
>
> You taste like
> salt and honeycomb,
> your lips like wine.

The Woman

2–3

The sun has set.
I've pulled off my clothes,
washed my feet,
and slipped into bed.

Lightning flashes in the night.
Rain thunders on the roof
and wakes me from a dream.

Listen—I hear you calling,
knocking at the door.

The Man

I fumble the key,
soaked by the storm,
battered by the wind.

The Woman

5

My heart beats wild
as the tumblers turn.

I'm through the door
and into the storm
before you know I'm there.

I kiss the rain from your eyes
and pull you stumbling
across the threshold.

You break my fall.

The Woman

I wake in the morning
to an empty bed.
I've lost you in the night.

I look for you everywhere,
but can't find you.
I call your name,
but no one answers.

Fear and shame overtake me.
Despair bruises me.
Naked and defenseless,
I need you.

Swear to me—
You will never stay lost.

Swear to me—
You will find me.

The Woman

5:10–
6:1

Across a crowded room,
I see you.

Your dark hair,
your shining eyes.

Your laughter rings
and lifts my heart.

I want to hear you laugh again.

At dinner, I rest my hand
lightly on your knee
and find any excuse
to lean close
and blush into your shoulder.

At the door,
I kiss you on tiptoes,
pulling your lips
down to mine.

You turn to leave—
but I haven't let go.

SONG OF SONGS 6

The Woman

2–3

You take me to the garden.
We gather lilies.
The night air is sharp
with the scent of blossoms.

You are mine
and I am yours
alone.

The Man

4–5

You are as beautiful
as a city shining in the morning sun,
as terrible as an army with banners.

Your eyes, so dark
and fierce and flashing.

The Man

I wake early and watch you sleep—

The lock of hair tucked behind your ear,
the laugh lines around your eyes,
your crooked tooth and parted lips,

how the sheet still clings
in the gray morning light
to the curve of your hip.

I lay my head on your breast and
listen to your heart,
your breath warm on my neck.

Again you stir and pull me close.

The Man

The world is crowded
with beautiful women.

You take my hand
and we head for the door.

The Woman

Who are you?

Who is this rising on the horizon,
bright as the sun,
clear as the moon,
fearless as the stars
in their courses?

The Man

11–12

I went down to the garden
to look for new flowers,
to see if the vines were climbing
and the pomegranates in bloom.

The Man

> You dance along the shore,
> the tide pulling at your feet,
> sandals damp,
> ankles spattered with sand.
>
> I squint into the morning sun,
> your dark figure
> haloed by light—
>
> straining wild hair
> from your bright eyes,
> a smile,
> strong shoulders,
> the turn of your breast,
> the angle of your hips,
> fleeting hands,
> the bend of your knee.
>
> You catch me staring
> and laugh.

6:13–
7:6

7–9   *The Man*

> The palm trees sway
> in the wind,
> heavy with fruit.
>
> Let me find rest
> in their shade.
>
> Let me find rest
> in your arms,
> my head at your breast,
> your kiss on my cheek,
> your touch like wine.

The Woman

I want you to wake
in the night,
burning,
and reach for me.

The Woman

Come with me into the fields
and we'll lie all night
in beds of flowering henna.

Come with me into the vineyard
and we'll stain our hands
with pomegranate seeds.

The air is filled
with the scent of mandrakes.

Come see what fruit
I've saved for you.

SONG OF SONGS 8

The Woman

    I want to lead you home
    to my mother's house.

    I want to kiss you
    in the streets,
    shamelessly.

    I want to serve you spiced wine.

The Woman

With one hand you cradle my head,
with one hand you pull me close.

Swear to me—
You won't wake love before its time.

The Woman

Back from the desert,
I remind you what promises
we made in the shade
of this apple tree.

You're quick to remember.

The Woman

6–7

Set me as a seal on your heart,
tie me like a prayer on your arm.

Love is fierce as death,
a raging fire against
the falling night.

No ocean is as vast,
no hunger as keen,
no promise as true.

It cannot be bought.

The Woman

In the mirror,
I never quite see
what you see.

Faltering,
I see in my eyes why
some build walls,
barricade the windows,
and lock the doors.

The Man

Unlike Solomon,
I have no wealth
or rolling vineyards
or armies at my command.

I have only this life,
this small lot,
my own heart and hands.

The Man

13

> Call for me.
> Let me hear your voice.

The Woman

14

Hurry—take my hand.
It's time.

Adam S. Miller is a professor of philosophy at Collin College in McKinney, Texas. He and his wife, Gwen, have three children. He is the author of *Badiou, Marion, and St Paul: Immanent Grace* (2008), *Rube Goldberg Machines: Essays in Mormon Theology* (2012), *Speculative Grace: Bruno Latour and Object-Oriented Theology* (2013), *Letters to a Young Mormon* (2014), *Grace is Not God's Backup Plan: An Urgent Paraphrase of Paul's Letter to the Romans* (2015), *Future Mormon: Essays in Mormon Theology* (2016), *Nothing New Under the Sun: A Blunt Paraphrase of Ecclesiastes* (2016), and *The Gospel According to David Foster Wallace: Boredom and Addiction in an Age of Distraction* (2016). He is also the editor of *An Experiment on the Word: Reading Alma 32* (2011), *A Dream, a Rock, and a Pillar of Fire: Reading 1 Nephi 1* (2017), and *Fleeing the Garden: Reading Genesis 2–3* (2017).

More at: www.adamsmiller.net

CPSIA information can be obtained
at www.ICGtesting.com
Printed in the USA
FSHW021259031219
64711FS